Knit Beanies

Easy to Make, Fun to Wear

Compiled by Karen M. Burns

Martingale
Create with Confidence

Knit Beanies: Easy to Make, Fun to Wear
© 2016 by Martingale & Company®

Martingale®
19021 120th Ave. NE, Ste. 102
Bothell, WA 98011-9511 USA
ShopMartingale.com

Printed in China
21 20 19 18 17 16   8 7 6 5 4 3 2 1

Library of Congress Cataloging-in-Publication Data
is available upon request.

ISBN: 978-1-60468-720-0

MISSION STATEMENT

We empower makers who use fabric and yarn to make life more enjoyable.

CREDITS

PUBLISHER AND
CHIEF VISIONARY OFFICER
Jennifer Erbe Keltner

CONTENT DIRECTOR
Karen Costello Soltys

MANAGING EDITOR
Tina Cook

ACQUISITIONS EDITOR
Karen M. Burns

TECHNICAL EDITOR
Amy Polcyn

COPY EDITOR
Tiffany Mottet

DESIGN MANAGER
Adrienne Smitke

PRODUCTION MANAGER
Regina Girard

COVER AND
INTERIOR DESIGNER
Connor Chin

PHOTOGRAPHER
Brent Kane

ILLUSTRATOR
Linda Schmidt

Contents

Get Ready for Some Stylish Knitting Fun!

Whether slouchy or close-fitting, knit beanies are fast to make and fun to wear. All you need is a skein of yarn and the right size knitting needles and you're in business. What's not to love about that?

In this book you'll find a variety of hats, some for each member of your family. Yep, there are hats for babies and toddlers, kids, and men and women. Some feature very basic stitches, making them perfect for beginning knitters, while others use a bit fancier stitches like cables, lace, or even colorwork.

If you're new to knitting in the round, many of the projects in this book are a perfect place to start. Knitting in rounds is just as easy as knitting back and forth in rows and there are no seams to sew in the end. So don't be intimidated by the circular nature of a beanie. You can whip up your first one in no time and be wearing it this weekend.

If you need help with your knitting stitches or getting started, you can simply visit our website, ShopMartingale.com/HowtoKnit, for free, illustrated information. We here at Martingale love to knit and we want you to enjoy it just as much as we do!

Karen Costello Soltys
Content Director

Whale

Your baby or child is bound to have a whale of a good time when out and about in this adorable beanie. The compliments are sure to come rolling in!

Designed by Megan Kreiner

Sizes: Newborn (Baby, Toddler, Child, Adult)

Skill Level: Intermediate ■■■□

Finished Circumference: 13 (14¾, 16½, 18½, 20)"

Materials

1 (1, 1, 1, 1) skein of Cascade Heritage 150 (75% superwash merino, 25% nylon; 5⅓ oz; 492 yds) (**1**) in each of the following colors:

MC: Anis

A: Snow

B: Real Black

US size 4 (3.5 mm) 16" circular needle and set of 5 double-pointed needles, or size needed to obtain gauge

Cable needle

Stitch marker

Tapestry needle

Polyester stuffing

Gauge

26 sts and 32 rows = 4" in St st

Special Abbreviation

C4B: Slip 2 sts to cable needle and hold in back, K2, K2 from cable needle.

Note

Hat begins at tip of waterspout and is worked from top down.

Hat

With circular needle and A, loosely CO 72 sts. PM and join, being careful not to twist sts.

Rnd 1 (beg waterspout): Knit.

Rnd 2: *K2tog 4 times, (YO, K1) 4 times; rep from * around—72 sts.

Rnd 3: *K4, P8; rep from * around.

Rnd 4: *C4B, K8; rep from * around.

Rnds 5–8: Rep rnds 1–4.

Rnd 9: *K2tog; rep from * around—36 sts. Change to dpn when needed.

Rnds 10–12: Purl.

Rnd 13: *P1, P2tog; rep from * around—24 sts.

Rnds 14 and 15: Purl.

Rnd 16: *P2tog; rep from * around—12 sts.

Rnds 17–23: Purl.

Cut A. Turn work inside out so rnds 10–23 have knit side facing you. Change to MC.

Rnd 24 (beg blowhole): Knit.

Rnd 25: *K1, M1; rep from * around—24 sts.

Rnd 26: Knit.

Rnd 27: *K1, M1, K1; rep from * around—36 sts.

Rnd 28: Knit.

Rnd 29: *K1, ssk; rep from * around—24 sts.

Rnd 30: Knit.

Rnd 31: *Ssk; rep from * around—12 sts.

Rnd 32: Knit.

Rnd 33 (beg hat body): *K1, M1; rep from * around—24 sts. Change to circular needle when needed.

Rnd 34: Knit.

Rnd 35: *K1, M1, K1; rep from * around—36 sts.

Rnd 36: Knit.

Rnd 37: *K1, M1, K2; rep from * around—48 sts.

Rnd 38: Knit.

Rnd 39: *K1, M1, K3; rep from * around—60 sts.

Rnd 40: Knit.

Rnd 41: *K1, M1, K4; rep from * around—72 sts.

Rnd 42: Knit.

Rnd 43: *K1, M1, K5; rep from * around—84 sts.

Rnd 44: Knit.

Newborn Size Only

Work even in St st until piece measures 4¾" from beg.

Baby–Adult Sizes Only

Rnd 45: *K1, M1, K6; rep from * around—96 sts.

Rnd 46: Knit.

Baby Size Only

Work even in St st until piece measures 5¾" from beg.

Toddler–Adult Sizes Only

Rnd 47: *K1, M1, K7; rep from * around—108 sts.

Rnd 48: Knit.

Toddler Size Only

Work even in St st until piece measures 6½" from beg.

Child and Adult Sizes Only

Rnd 49: *K1, M1, K8; rep from * around—120 sts.

Rnd 50: Knit.

Child Size Only

Work even in St st until piece measures 7" from beg.

Adult Size Only

Rnd 51: *K1, M1, K9; rep from * 11 more times—132 sts.

Rnd 52: Knit.

Work even in St st until piece measures 7½" from beg.

All Sizes

Cut MC. Change to A. Purl 4 rnds. Do not BO. Set aside.

Band

With dpn and A, loosely CO 84 (96, 108, 120, 132) sts. Divide sts on needles, taking care to have a multiple of 8 sts on each.

Rnd 1: Knit.

Rnd 2: *K2tog 4 times, (YO, K1) 4 times; rep from * around—84 (96, 108, 120, 132) sts.

Rnd 3: *K4, P8; rep from * around.

Rnd 4: *C4B, K8; rep from * around.

Rep rnds 1–4 a total of 1 (2, 2, 3, 3) more times. Cut yarn, leaving a 24" tail. Do not BO.

Finishing

Align sts of band and hat, RS facing you and band against body of hat. With A, join using Kitchener st (page 61).

With tapestry needle and MC, sew rnd 24 to rnd 32 of hat to shape outer edge of blowhole. Stuff lightly. With tapestry needle and A, apply a running stitch through rnd 16 of spout, pull tightly to gather, and secure. Sew in place on blowhole.

Front Flippers

Make 2.

With dpn and MC, CO 6 sts. PM and join, being careful not to twist the sts.

Rnd 1: *Kfb, K1, Kfb; rep from * around—10 sts.

Rnd 2: Knit.

Rnd 3: K1, *M1, K1; rep from * 3 more times, K1, **M1, K1; rep from ** 3 more times—18 sts.

Rnds 4–10: Knit.

Rnd 11: *K1, K2tog; rep from * around—12 sts.

Rnd 12: Knit.

Stuff lightly.

Rnd 13: *K1, K2tog; rep from * around—8 sts.

Rnd 14: Knit.

BO all sts.

Tail Fins

Make 2.

With dpn and A, CO 5 sts.

Row 1 (RS): K1 *M1, K1; rep from * 3 more times—9 sts.

Row 2: Purl.

Row 3: (K1, M1R) 2 times, K2, M1R, K1, M1L, K2, (M1L, K1) 2 times—15 sts.

Row 4: Purl.

Row 5: (K1, M1R) 2 times, K5, M1R, K1, M1L, K5, (M1L, K1) 2 times—21 sts.

Row 6: Purl.

Row 7: (K1, M1R) 2 times, K8, M1R, K1, M1L, K8, (M1L, K1) 2 times—27 sts.

Row 8: Purl.

Row 9: (K1, M1R) 2 times, K11, M1R, K1, M1L, K11, (M1L, K1) 2 times—33 sts.

Row 10: Purl.

Row 11: K1, M1R, K15, M1R, K1, M1L, K15, M1L, K1—37 sts.

Rows 12–14: Work in St st.

Row 15: Ssk, K14, K2tog, turn and work only these 16 sts.

Row 16: P2tog, P14—15 sts.

BO.

With RS facing up, rejoin yarn, working on rem 19 sts.

Row 17: BO 1 st, sl BO st from right needle to left, ssk, K14, K2tog.

Row 18: P14, P2tog—15 sts.

BO.

Assembly

Sew tail pieces together with RS facing you, stuffing before closing seam. Apply a running stitch along center of the tail to define. Sew tail to hat as shown. Sew front flippers in place. With B, embroider eyes.

Weave in ends. Block.

Cat Hat

Your child can be at the height of animal-hat fashion with this black-cat knitted hat. Or, change up the color scheme to coordinate with your favorite kitty.

Designed by Violette Lovelace Skill Level: Easy ■■□□ Size: Child Finished Circumference: 18" (stretches to fit)

Materials

1 skein of Bernat Softee Chunky
(100% acrylic; 3½ oz; 108 yds)
(6) in each of the following
colors:

MC: Black

CC: Baby Pink

US size 10 (6 mm) 16" circular
needle and set of 5 double-
pointed needles, *or* size
needed to obtain gauge

US size J-10 (6 mm) crochet hook

Stitch marker

Stitch holders

Tapestry needle

Gauge

12 sts and 16 rows = 4" in St st

Earflaps

Make 2.

With MC, CO 5 sts.

Rows 1 and 2: Knit.

Rows 3, 5, 7, 9, and 11 (RS):
K1, Kfb, knit to last 2 sts, Kfb,
K1—15 sts.

Rows 4, 6, 8, 10, and 12: Knit.

Cut yarn, leaving a 12" tail.
Place sts on a holder or spare
needle.

Hat

With circular needle, CO 12 sts.
Knit across first earflap, CO 12
more sts, knit across second
earflap. PM and join, being
careful not to twist the sts—
54 sts.

Work 12 rnds even in St st.

Shape Crown

Change to dpn when needed.

Rnd 1: K2tog, K7; rep from *
around—48 sts.

**Rnds 2 and all even-numbered
rnds:** Knit.

Rnd 3: K2tog, K6; rep from *
around—42 sts.

Rnd 5: K2tog, K5; rep from *
around—36 sts.

Rnd 7: K2tog, K4; rep from *
around—30 sts.

Rnd 9: K2tog, K3; rep from *
around—24 sts.

Rnd 11: K2tog, K2; rep from *
around—18 sts.

Rnd 13: K2tog, K1; rep from *
around—12 sts.

Rnd 14: K2tog; rep from *
around—6 sts.

Cut yarn, draw through rem sts,
pull tight and secure. Weave in
ends.

Ears

With CC, CO 1 st.

Row 1 (RS): Kfb—2 sts.

**Row 2 and all even-numbered
rows:** Purl.

Row 3: Kfb twice—4 sts.

Row 5: Kfb, K2, Kfb—6 sts.

Row 7: Kfb, K4, Kfb—8 sts.

Row 9: Kfb, K6, Kfb—10 sts.

Row 10: Cut CC, leaving a 12"
tail. Change to MC, leave a
12" tail, and purl across.

Rows 11 and 19: Work in St st.

Row 13: K2tog, K6, K2tog—8 sts.

Row 15: K2tog, K4, K2tog—6 sts.

Row 17: K2tog, K2, K2tog—4 sts.

Row 18: K2tog twice—2 sts.

Row 20: K2tog—1 st.

Cut yarn, draw through rem st
and secure.

Finishing

With tail of CC, sew sides of ear
tog. With tail of MC, sew finished
ear to hat along decrease above
earflap.

With crochet hook and MC, work
1 rnd of single crochet along
lower edges and earflaps.

Ties (Optional)

With MC, pick up and knit 5 sts
from CO edge of earflap. Work in
garter st (knit every row) for 15"
or desired length. Bind off. Rep
on other earflap.

Weave in ends.

Chevron Color Pop

The focus is on stripes in this quick-to-knit beanie.
Make one for a baby or toddler and make one to match for
yourself! Choose school colors, favorite sports-team colors,
or simply your favorite color palette.

Designed by Jessica Anderson
Sizes: Newborn (Baby, Toddler, Child, Adult)
Skill Level: Easy ■■□□
Finished Circumference: 12½ (14¼, 16, 17¾, 20½)"

Materials

1 (1, 1, 1, 1) skein of Lion Brand Vanna's Choice (100% acrylic; 3½ oz; 170 yds) (**4**) in each of the following colors:

- MC: Cranberry
- A: Silver Grey
- B: Black

US size 7 (4.5 mm) 16" circular needle and set of 5 double-pointed needles, *or* size needed to obtain gauge

Stitch marker

Tapestry needle

Gauge

18 sts and 24 rows = 4" in St st

Hat

With circular needle and B, CO 56 (64, 72, 80, 92) sts. PM and join, being careful not to twist sts. Work in K2, P2 rib for 1".

Rnd 1: Knit.

Rnds 2 and 3: With A, knit.

Rnds 4 and 5: With MC, knit.

Rnds 6 and 7: With A, knit.

Rnds 8 and 9: With MC, knit.

Rnd 10: Knit, inc 10 (2, 10, 2, 6) sts evenly around—66 (66, 82, 82, 98) sts.

Rnd 11: Knit.

Rnd 12: With B, K1, ssk, *K12, K2tog, ssk; rep from * until 15 sts rem, K12, K2tog, K1—58 (58, 72, 72, 86) sts.

Rnd 13: P7; *Pfb, Pfb, P12; rep from * until 9 sts rem, Pfb, Pfb, P7—66 (66, 82, 82, 98) sts.

Rnds 14–19: Rep rnds 12 and 13—66 (66, 82, 82, 98) sts after rnd 19.

With MC, work in St st until piece measures 4½ (5, 5½, 6, 7)" from beg.

Shape Crown

Change to dpn when needed.

Rnd 1: *K9, K2tog; rep from * around, ending K0 (0, 5, 5, 10)—60 (60, 75, 75, 90) sts.

Rnd 2: Knit.

Rnd 3: *K8, K2tog; rep from * around, ending K0 (0, 5, 5, 0)—54 (54, 68, 68, 81) sts.

Rnd 4: *K7, K2tog; rep from * around, ending K0 (0, 5, 5, 0)—48 (48, 61, 61, 72) sts.

Rnd 5: Knit.

Rnd 6: *K6, K2tog; rep from * around, ending K0 (0, 5, 5, 0)—42 (42, 54, 54, 63) sts.

Rnd 7: *K5, K2tog; rep from * around, ending K0 (0, 5, 5, 0)—36 (36, 47, 47, 54) sts.

Rnd 8: *K4, K2tog; rep from * around, ending K0 (0, [K2tog twice, K1], [K2tog twice, K1], K0)—30 (30, 38, 38, 45) sts.

Rnd 9: *K3, K2tog; rep from * around, ending K0 (0, [K2tog, K1], [K2tog, K1], K0)—24 (24, 30, 30, 36) sts.

Rnd 10: *K2, K2tog; rep from * around, ending K0 (0, K2tog, K2tog, K0)—18 (18, 22, 22, 27) sts.

Rnd 11: *K1, K2tog; rep from * around, ending K0 (0, 1, 1, 0)—12 (12, 15, 15, 18) sts.

Rnd 12: *K2tog; rep from * around, ending K0 (0, 1, 1, 0)—6 (6, 8, 8, 9) sts.

Cut yarn, draw through rem sts, pull tight and secure.

Finishing

Weave in ends. Block lightly.

Portland Birdie

Ramp up your knitting with this adorable colorwork beanie for baby and child. Boys and girls alike will look so cute with a stuffed little bird perched atop a pom-pom nest.

Designed by Megan Kreiner   Skill Level: Intermediate ■■■□   Sizes: Baby (Toddler, Child)   Finished Circumference: 16½ (18½, 20)"

Materials

1 (1, 1) skein of Cascade Heritage 150 (75% superwash merino, 25% nylon; 5⅓ oz; 492 yds) **1** in each of the following colors:

MC: Burgundy
  A: Anemone
  B: Anis
  C: Como Blue
  D: Snow
  E: Camel
  F: Real Black

US size 4 (3.5 mm) 16" circular needle and set of 5 double-pointed needles, or size needed to obtain gauge
Stitch marker
Tapestry needle
Polyester stuffing
Scrap of cardboard, 3" long

Gauge

26 sts and 32 rows = 4" in St st

Stitch Pattern

See chart on page 16.

Hat

With circular needle and MC, CO 108 (120, 132) sts. PM and join, being careful not to twist sts.

Rnd 1: *K4, P2; rep from * around.

Rnds 2 and 3: Rep rnd 1.

Rnd 4: Change to A, rep rnd 1.

Rnd 5: Change to MC, rep rnd 1.

Rnd 6: Change to A, rep rnd 1.

Rnds 7–9: Change to MC, rep rnd 1.

Knit 2, (3, 4) rnds even.

Work 12-st rep of chart 9 (10, 11) times until all 28 rnds have been completed.

With MC, work even in St st until piece measures 5¼ (5¾, 6¾)" from beg.

Shape Crown

Child Size Only

Rnd 1: *K9, ssk; rep from * 11 times—120 sts.

Rnds 2 and 3: Knit.

Toddler and Child Sizes Only

Rnd 1: *K8, ssk; rep from * 11 times—108 sts.

Rnds 2 and 3: Knit.

All Sizes

Change to dpn when needed.

Rnd 1: *K7, K2tog; rep from * around—96 sts.

Rnd 2: Knit.

Rnd 3: *K6, K2tog; rep from * around—84 sts.

Rnd 4: Knit.

Rnd 5: *K5, K2tog; rep from * around—72 sts.

Rnd 6: *K4, K2tog; rep from * around—60 sts.

Rnd 7: *K3, K2tog; rep from * around—48 sts.

Rnd 8: *K2, K2tog; rep from * around—36 sts.

Rnd 9: *K1, K2tog; rep from * around—24 sts.

Rnd 10: *K2tog; rep from * around—12 sts.

Cut yarn, draw through rem sts, pull tight and secure.

Finishing

Weave in ends.

Stranding Tips

It's vital to work the stranding on this hat as loosely as possible to prevent puckering. Here are some tips for doing just that:

- Keep your stitches spread out on the needles as you work.
- Turn the hat inside out as you work. You'll work the pattern the same way, but your floats will be on the outside of your work as you go, adding some extra slack in the yarn.
- Block the hat when complete to smooth out minor puckers. To block, lay the hat flat, straighten out the hat band, and cover it with a towel. Steam through the towel with an iron on the "wool" setting. Turn the hat over and repeat on the other side.

Bird

With D, CO 6 sts. PM and join, being careful not to twist sts.

Rnd 1: *Kfb; rep from * around—12 sts.

Rnd 2: Knit.

Rnd 3: *K2, M1, K1; rep from * around—16 sts.

Rnd 4: Knit.

Rnd 5: *K3, M1, K1; rep from * around—20 sts.

Rnd 6: Knit.

Rnd 7: *K4, M1, K1; rep from * around—24 sts.

Rnd 8: Knit.

Rnd 9: *K5, M1, K1; rep from * around—28 sts.

Rnds 10 and 11: Knit.

Change to A.

Rnd 12: Knit.

Rnd 13: *K5, K2tog; rep from * around—24 sts.

Rnd 14: Knit.

Rnd 15: *K2, K2tog; rep from * around—18 sts.

Rnd 16: Knit.

Change to B.

Rnd 17: *K8, M1, K1; rep from * around—20 sts.

Rnd 18: Knit.

Rnd 19: *K3, K2tog; rep from * around—16 sts.

Rnd 20: Knit.

Rnd 21: *K6, K2tog; rep from * around—14 sts.

Rnd 22: Knit.

Rnd 23: *K5, K2tog; rep from * around—12 sts.

Rnd 24: Knit.

Stuff. Cut yarn, draw through rem sts, pull tight and secure.

Tail and Back

With C, CO 12 sts. PM and join, being careful not to twist sts.

Rnd 1: Knit.

Rnd 2: *K1, K2tog; rep from * around—8 sts.

Rnds 3 and 4: Knit.

Rnd 5: *K2, K2tog; rep from * around—6 sts.

Rnds 6 and 7: Knit.

Rnd 8: BO 2 sts, slip BO st from right needle to left, Kfb 4 times—8 sts.

Beg working back and forth in rows.

Row 9 (WS): Purl.

Row 10: Kfb 8 times—16 sts.

Row 11: Purl.

Row 12: *K1, M1R; rep from * 1 time, K12, **M1L, K1; rep from ** 1 time—20 sts.

Rows 13–17: Work in St st.

Row 18: *K1, ssk, K14, K2tog, K1—18 sts.

Row 19: Purl.

Row 20: BO 2 sts, knit to end— 16 sts.

Row 21: BO 2 sts, purl to end— 14 sts.

Row 22: K1, ssk 3 times, K2tog 3 times, K1—8 sts.

Row 23: Purl.

Row 24: K1, ssk, K2, K2tog, K1—6 sts.

Row 25: Purl.

Row 26: K1, ssk, K2tog, K1—4 sts.

Cut yarn, draw through rem sts, pull tight and secure.

Wings

Make 2.

With C, CO 5 sts.

Row 1 (RS): Kfb 5 times—10 sts.

Row 2: Purl.

Row 3: (K1, M1) twice, K6, (M1, K1) twice—14 sts.

Row 4: Purl.

Row 5: Ssk 3 times, K2, K2tog 3 times—8 sts.

Row 6: Purl.

Row 7: Ssk 2 times, K2tog 2 times—4 sts.

Row 8: Purl.

Cut yarn, draw through rem sts, pull tight and secure. Sew edges together.

Assemble Bird and Nest

Position tail and back piece on bird body with last row above middle of bird's face, with corners created by bound-off sts on rows

20 and 21 lined up with first round of B on body. Sew in place. Sew seam at end of tail. Sew wings in place.

With E, embroider beak as shown in photo on page 14. With F, work French knots for eyes.

Nest Pom-Pom

Wrap E around a scrap of 3"-long cardboard approx 100 times. Tie firmly around center on each side, slide off cardboard, tie both pieces together in center, and cut loops at each end. Tie entire piece together in center, trim ends, and fluff. Sew to bird, and then sew entire assembly to top of hat.

Bird in Nest

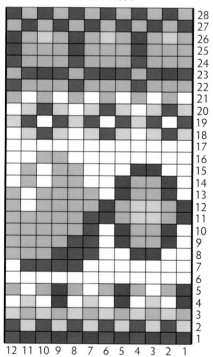

Repeat = 12 sts

Legend

MC: Burgundy

A: Anemone

B: Anis

C: Como Blue

D: Snow

E: Camel

Fiddlehead Fern

Worked from the top down and starting with the main color and fiddlehead fern I-cord, you can change colors for each band of contrast purl stitches or make them all matching. This project is great for using up leftovers.

Designed by David Owen Hastings

Sizes: Newborn (Baby)

Finished Circumference: 12 (14½)"

Materials

1 (1) skein of Cascade 220 Heathers (100% wool; 3½ oz; 220 yds) 🄴 in each of the following colors: *

   MC: Turtle

    A: Dune

    B: Bronzed Green

    C: Sparrow

US size 6 (4 mm) 16" circular needle and set of 5 double-pointed needles, or size needed to obtain gauge

Stitch marker

Tapestry needle

If you start with full skeins of Cascade 220 Heather yarns in four as shown here, you'll have enough to make four or more hats, so be sure to check out the Jester variation on page 19.

Gauge

20 sts and 28 rows = 4" in St st

Special Technique

I-Cord: With dpn, *knit 1 row; without turning work, slide sts to right end of needle; rep from * until cord measures desired length.

I-Cord Topper

With MC, CO 5 sts on 1 dpn, leaving a 6" tail. Work in I-cord until piece measures approx 8".

Next row: K1, M1, K4—6 sts. Do not cut yarn.

Hat

Divide sts evenly on 3 dpn. PM and join, being careful not to twist sts. Change to circular needle when needed.

Rnd 1: *Kfb; rep from * around—12 sts.

Rnd 2 and all even-numbered rnds through 18: Knit.

Rnd 3: *Kfb, K1; rep from * around—18 sts.

Rnd 5: *Kfb, K2; rep from * around—24 sts.

Rnd 7: *Kfb, K3; rep from * around—30 sts.

Rnd 9: *Kfb, K4; rep from * around—36 sts.

Rnd 11: *Kfb, K5; rep from * around—42 sts.

Rnd 13: *Kfb, K6; rep from * around—48 sts.

Rnd 15: *Kfb, K7; rep from * around—54 sts.

Rnd 17: *Kfb, K8; rep from * around—60 sts.

Baby Size Only

Rnd 19: *Kfb, K9; rep from * around—66 sts.

Rnd 20: Knit.

Rnd 21: *Kfb, K10; rep from * around—72 sts.

All Sizes

Change to A. Knit 1 rnd. Purl 3 rnds. Change to MC. Knit 4 rnds.

Rep from * to *, using B instead of A on next rep, then C on following rep.

Change to MC. Knit 12 (16) rnds more. BO loosely.

Changing Colors

When changing yarns, try the slipknot method to join. Create a loose slipknot in the new yarn, leaving a 4" tail. Put the tail of the old yarn through the loop. Position the loose slipknot close to the last stitch. Holding the new yarn on both sides of the slipknot, pull the yarn ends away from each other quickly. You should feel a little "pop" as the old yarn gets trapped in a knot by the new yarn. If it doesn't pop, pull off the slipknot and try again.

Finishing

Gently roll I-cord on top of hat in a loose spiral as shown. Tack in place. Weave in ends.

Jester Beanie Variation

I-cords

Make 6.

With desired color, CO 5 sts on 1 dpn, leaving a 6" tail. Work in I-cord until piece measures approx 1½" to 2".

Next row: K2tog, K3tog—2 sts. Cut yarn.

Place all cords on dpn tog—12 sts.

Next rnd: With MC, *K2tog; rep from * around—6 sts. PM and join, being careful not to twist the sts. Finish as for Fiddlehead Fern Beanie, omitting sewing I-cord in place at end.

Just for Fun

*Little girls—and big girls too—*will be happy to
wear this hat adorned with a field of colorful bobbles
above heavy ridge stripes and squiggles shooting from
the top corners. When subtle just won't do, pull on
"Just for Fun" and bring out the smiles.

Designed by Sheryl Thies   Skill Level: Easy ■■□□

Sizes: Baby (Toddler, Child)

Finished Circumference: 15¾ (17, 18½)"

Materials

Dale Freestyle (100% pure new wool; 1¾ oz; 87 yds) [4] in the following amounts and colors:

MC: 1 (2, 2) skeins Neon Pink

A: 1 skein Neon Green

B: 1 skein Neon Yellow

C: 1 skein Neon Orange

US size 8 (5 mm) straight needles, or size needed to obtain gauge

Stitch marker

Tapestry needle

Gauge

18 sts = 4" in Ridge patt

Special Abbreviation

MB: Knit in front, back and front of next st, turn, P3, turn, K3, turn, P3, turn, sl 1-K2tog-psso.

Ridge Pattern

Row 1 (RS): Knit.

Row 2: Purl.

Row 3: K1, *Kfb; rep from * to last st, K1.

Row 4: K1, *K2tog; rep from * to last st, K1.

Rep rows 1–4 for patt.

Bobble Pattern

Row 1 (RS): With MC, K6; *with B, MB; with MC, K5; rep from * across, end K1. Cut B.

Rows 2, 4, and 6: With MC, purl.

Row 3: With MC, K3; *with C, MB; with MC, K5; rep from * across, end with C, MB; with MC, K3. Cut C.

Row 5: With MC, K6, *with A, MB; with MC, K5; rep from * across, end K1. Cut A.

Row 7: Rep row 3.

Row 8: With MC, purl.

Rep rows 1–8 for patt.

Hat

With A, loosely CO 71 (77, 83) sts. Knit 1 row.

Next row (RS): K1, *Kfb; rep from * to last st, K1—140 (152, 164) sts.

Next row: K1, *K2tog; rep from * to last st, K1—71 (77, 83) sts.

With B, work rows 1–4 of Ridge patt once.

With C, work rows 1–4 of Ridge patt once.

With A, work rows 1–4 of Ridge patt once.

Next row (RS): With MC, K1, Kfb, knit to last 2 sts, Kfb, K1—73 (79, 85) sts.

Purl one row.

Work in Bobble patt until piece measures 7¼ (7¾, 8¼)", ending with a WS row.

Knit one row.

Purl one row.

BO loosely.

Finishing

Bring sides together and sew back seam. Fold so back seam is centered and seam along top of hat. Weave in ends.

Corner Embellishments

Make 2 in each of colors A, B, and C.

With A, CO 16 sts loosely and BO tightly. Cut yarn, leaving 6" tail.

With B, CO 15 sts loosely and BO tightly. Cut yarn, leaving 6" tail.

With C, CO 18 sts loosely and BO tightly. Cut yarn, leaving 6" tail.

Insert 3 embellishments in each top corner and fasten tails securely on inside of hat.

Block lightly.

Garter Flap Cap

Quick to knit and fun to wear, this earflap hat will keep your child cozy when it's cold outside. The pattern is for three sizes, so you can knit for baby and big kids alike.

Designed by Doreen L. Marquart

Skill Level: Easy ■■□□

Sizes: Baby (Toddler, Child)

Finished Circumference: 16 (18½, 20)"

Materials

1 (1, 1) skein of Malabrigo Rios (100% superwash merino; 3½ oz; 210 yds) (4) in color Arco Iris

US size 7 (4.5 mm) 16" circular needle and set of 5 double-pointed needles, or size needed to obtain gauge

Stitch marker

Tapestry needle

Gauge

20 sts and 36 rows = 4" in garter st

Special Technique

I-Cord: With dpn, *knit 1 row; without turning work, slide sts to right end of needle; rep from * until cord measures desired length.

Ties and Earflaps

Make 2.

With dpn, CO 4 sts. Work 8 (9, 10)" in I-cord for ties.

Continue earflap section as follows:

Row 1 (RS): K1, Kfb, K2—5 sts.

Row 2 and all even-numbered rows: Knit.

Rows 3, 5, 7, and 9: Kfb, knit to last 2 sts, Kfb, K1—13 sts.

Row 11: Knit.

Row 13: Kfb, knit to last 2 sts, Kfb, K1—15 sts.

Row 15: Knit.

Row 17: Kfb, knit to last 2 sts, Kfb, K1—17 sts.

Rows 19 and 20: Knit.

Baby Size Only

Knit 6 rows even.

Toddler Size Only

Row 21: Kfb, knit to last 2 sts, Kfb, K1—19 sts.

Row 22: Knit.

Knit 8 rows even.

Child Size Only

Row 21: Kfb, knit to last 2 sts, Kfb, K1—19 sts.

Row 22: Knit.

Row 23: Kfb, knit to last 2 sts, Kfb, K1—21 sts.

Row 24: Knit.

Knit 10 rows even.

All Sizes

Cut yarn, slip earflap onto spare dpn. Rep for second earflap. Set aside.

Hat

With circular needle, CO 80 (92, 100) sts. PM and join, being careful not to twist sts.

Knit 8 (10, 12) rnds.

Next (joining) rnd: K8 (9, 10); place one set of earflap sts behind body of hat sts (with RS of each facing you); knit next 17 (19, 21) sts from hat body, knitting each stitch tog with appropriate st from earflap to join; K30 (36, 38) sts; place second set of earflap sts behind hat body sts, knit next 17 (19, 21) sts from hat body, joining earflap as before; knit rem 8 (9, 10) sts. PM to mark beg of rnd.

Work even in garter st (knit one rnd, purl one rnd) for 3¾ (4, 4½)", ending with a purl rnd.

Shape Crown

Change to dpn when needed.

Rnd 1: *K2tog tbl, K16 (19, 21), K2tog; rep from * around—72 (84, 92) sts.

Rnd 2 and all even-numbered rnds: Purl.

Rnd 3: *K2tog tbl, K14 (17, 19), K2tog; rep from * around—64 (76, 84) sts.

Rnd 5: *K2tog tbl, K12 (15, 17), K2tog; rep from * around—56 (68, 76) sts.

Rnd 7: *K2tog tbl, K10 (13, 15), K2tog; rep from * around—48 (60, 68) sts.

Rnd 9: *K2tog tbl, K8 (11, 13), K2tog; rep from * around—40 (52, 60) sts.

Rnd 11: *K2tog tbl, K6 (9, 11), K2tog; rep from * around—32 (44, 52) sts.

Rnd 13: *K2tog tbl, K4 (7, 9), K2tog; rep from * around—24 (36, 44) sts.

Rnd 15: *K2tog tbl, K2 (5, 7), K2tog; rep from * around—16 (28, 36) sts.

Rnd 17: *K2tog tbl, K0 (3, 5), K2tog; rep from * around—8 (20, 28) sts.

Baby Size Only

Cut yarn, draw through rem sts, pull tight and secure.

Toddler and Child Sizes Only

Rnd 18: Purl.

Rnd 19: *K2tog tbl, K1 (3), K2tog; rep from * around—12 (20) sts.

Toddler Size Only

Cut yarn, draw through rem sts, pull tight and secure.

Child Size Only

Rnd 20: Purl.

Rnd 21: *K2tog tbl, K1, K2tog; rep from * around—12 sts.

Cut yarn, draw through rem sts, pull tight and secure.

Finishing

Weave in ends. Block.

Oh Nuts

When the cooler air arrives in fall, this acorn lace hat will become a perennial favorite. Acorns symbolize prosperity and success. Stay warm and maximize your good luck. Add an acorn tassel for a touch more good fortune.

Designed by Sheryl Thies   Skill Level: Intermediate ■■■□   Sizes: Adult Small (Large)   Finished Circumference: 21 (22½)"

Materials

1 skein of Done Roving Yarns Frolicking Feet (100% domestic superwash merino; 4 oz; 480 yds) (**1**) in color Cherry Pits

US size 6 (4 mm) 16" circular needle and set of 5 double-pointed needles, *OR* size needed to obtain gauge

US size 3 (3.25mm) straight needles (for acorn tassel)

Stitch marker

Tapestry needle

Gauge

16 sts = 4" in St st with larger needles and yarn held double

Acorn Lace

See chart on page 27.

Rnds 1 and 2: *K3, P3; rep from * around.

Rnd 3: *YO, K3tog, YO, K3; rep from * around.

Rnd 4: *P1, K1, P1, K3; rep from * around.

Rnds 5 and 6: *P3, K3; rep from * around.

Rnd 7: *K3, YO, K3tog, YO; rep from * around.

Rnd 8: *K3, P1, K1, P1; rep from * around.

Rep rnds 1–8 for patt.

Hat

With larger circular needle and 2 strands of yarn held together, loosely CO 84 (90) sts. PM and join, being careful not to twist sts. Work in K3, P3 rib for 1".

Work even in Acorn Lace patt until piece measures 7 (8)", ending with either rnd 2 or 6.

Knit 2 rnds.

Purl 3 rnds.

Shape Crown

Change to dpn when needed.

Rnd 1: *K12 (13), K2tog; rep from * around—78 (84) sts.

Rnd 2 and all even-numbered rnds through rnd 22: Knit.

Rnd 3: *K11 (12), K2tog; rep from * around—72 (78) sts.

Rnd 5: *K10 (11), K2tog; rep from * around—66 (72) sts.

Rnd 7: *K9 (10), K2tog; rep from * around—60 (66) sts.

Rnd 9: *K8 (9), K2tog; rep from * around—54 (60) sts.

Rnd 11: *K7 (8), K2tog; rep from * around—48 (54) sts.

Rnd 13: *K6 (7), K2tog; rep from * around—42 (48) sts.

Rnd 15: *K5 (6), K2tog; rep from * around—36 (42) sts.

Rnd 17: *K4 (5), K2tog; rep from * around—30 (36) sts.

Rnd 19: *K3 (4), K2tog; rep from * around—24 (30) sts.

Rnd 21: *K2 (3), K2tog; rep from * around—18 (24) sts.

Rnd 23: *K1 (2), K2tog; rep from * around—12 (18) sts.

Large Size Only

Rnd 24: Knit.

Rnd 25: *K1, K2tog; rep from * around—12 sts.

All Sizes

Cut yarn, draw through rem sts, pull tight and secure.

Finishing

Weave in ends. Block lightly.

Acorn Tassels

Make 3.

With smaller needles and a single strand of yarn, CO 5 sts, leaving a 12" tail.

Row 1 (RS): *Kfb; rep from * across—10 sts.

Rows 2, 4, 6, and 8: Purl.

Rows 3, 5, and 7: Knit.

Row 9: K1, *Kfb; rep from * to last st, K1—18 sts.

Rows 10–14: Knit.

Row 15: *K2tog; rep from * across—9 sts.

Row 16: *K2tog; rep from * to last st, K1—5 sts.

Cut yarn, draw through rem sts, pull tight and secure.

With tail at CO edge, sew seam toward acorn cap. Tie starting and ending tails together at top of acorn.

Hold tails from 3 acorns together and insert in center top of hat. Adjust length to suit and secure. Weave in ends. Block.

Oh Nuts

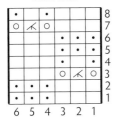

Repeat = 6 sts

Legend

☐ K on RS, P on WS

• P on RS, K on WS

○ YO

⚰ K3tog

Cables and Lace

Cables and lace make this hat fun to knit.
The beginning rib flows into the stitch pattern while the
crown decreases flow out of the pattern, giving the hat
a crisp, clean look. The pattern is written for five sizes,
meaning you can make one for everyone you know!

Designed by Jen Lucas

Sizes: Baby (Toddler, Child, Adult Small, Adult Large)

Skill Level: Intermediate ■■■□

Finished Circumference: 14 (16, 18, 20, 22)"

Materials

1 (1, 1, 1, 2) skeins of The Fibre Company Road to China Light (65% baby alpaca, 10% cashmere, 10% camel, 15% silk; 1¾ oz; 159 yds) 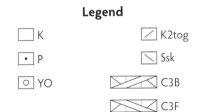, in color Blue Tourmaline

US size 3 (3.25 mm) 16" circular needle and set of 5 double-pointed needles, or size needed to obtain gauge

Stitch marker

Cable needle

Tapestry needle

Gauge

24 sts and 36 rows = 4" in St st

Special Abbreviations

C3B: Slip 2 sts to cable needle and hold in back, K1, K2 from cable needle.

C3F: Slip 1 st to cable needle and hold in front, K2, K1 from cable needle.

Stitch Pattern

See chart at right.

Rnd 1: *C3B, C3F, P1, YO, ssk, K2tog, YO, P1; rep from * around.

Rnd 2: *K6, P1, K4, P1; rep from * around.

Rnd 3: *K6, P1, YO, ssk, K2tog, YO, P1; rep from * around.

Rnd 4: Rep rnd 2.

Rep rnds 1–4 for patt.

Hat

With circular needle, CO 84 (96, 108, 120, 132) sts. PM and join, being careful not to twist sts.

Rnd 1: *K2, P2, K2, P1, K4, P1; rep from * around.

Rep rnd 1 for another 11 (11, 14, 17, 17) rnds.

Work rnds 1–4 of stitch patt 5 (8, 9, 10, 12) times total—20 (32, 36, 40, 48) rnds. Work rnds 1 and 2 of patt once more.

Shape Crown

Change to dpn when needed.

Rnd 1: *Ssk, K2, K2tog, P1, YO, ssk, K2tog, YO, P1; rep from * around—70 (80, 90, 100, 110) sts.

Rnd 2: *K4, P1; rep from * around.

Rnd 3: *Ssk, K2tog, P1, YO, ssk, K2tog, YO, P1; rep from * around—56 (64, 72, 80, 88) sts.

Rnd 4: *K2, P1, K4, P1; rep from * around.

Rnd 5: *Ssk, P1, YO, ssk, K2tog, YO, P1; rep from * around—49 (56, 63, 70, 77) sts.

Rnd 6: *K1, P1, K4, P1; rep from * around.

Rnd 7: *K1, P1, ssk, K2tog, P1; rep from * around—35 (40, 45, 50, 55) sts.

Rnd 8: *K1, P1, K2, P1; rep from * around.

Rnd 9: *K1, P1, K2tog, P1; rep from * around—28 (32, 36, 40, 44) sts.

Rnd 10: *K2tog; rep from * around—14 (16, 18, 20, 22) sts.

Rnd 11: Rep rnd 10—7 (8, 9, 10, 11) sts.

Cut yarn, draw through rem sts, pull tight and secure.

Finishing

Weave in ends. Block.

Cable & Lace

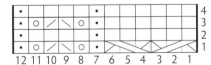

Repeat = 12 sts

Legend

☐	K	╱	K2tog
•	P	╲	Ssk
○	YO	⧅	C3B
		⧄	C3F

Swirl

Featuring a simple stitch pattern with just one row
to memorize, this hat works up quickly with chunky yarn.

Designed by Amy Polcyn Niezur

Skill Level: Easy ■■□□

Size: Adult

Finished Circumference: 19½" (stretches to fit)

Materials

1 skein of Berroco Lodge (47% wool, 47% acrylic, 6% rayon; 1¾ oz; 98 yds) **5** in color Sequoia

US size 10 (6 mm) 16" circular and set of 5 double-pointed needles, or size needed to obtain gauge

Stitch marker

Tapestry needle

Gauge

15 sts and 20 rows = 4" in patt

Stitch Pattern

*Ssk, K4, YO, K2; rep from * around.

Rep for patt.

Hat

With circular needle, CO 72 sts. PM and join, being careful not to twist sts. Work in K1 tbl, P1 rib for 1½". Change to stitch patt and work even until piece measures 6" from beg.

Shape Crown

Change to dpn when needed.

Rnd 1: *Sl 1-K2tog-psso, K3, YO, K2; rep from * around—63 sts.

Rnd 2: *Ssk, K3, YO, K2; rep from * around.

Rnd 3: *Sl 1-K2tog-psso, K2, YO, K2; rep from * around—54 sts.

Rnd 4: *Ssk, K2, YO, K2; rep from * around.

Rnd 5: *Sl 1-K2tog-psso, K1, YO, K2; rep from * around—45 sts.

Rnd 6: *Ssk, K1, YO, K2; rep from * around.

Rnd 7: *Sl 1-K2tog-psso, YO, K2; rep from * around—36 sts.

Rnd 8: *Ssk, YO, K2; rep from * around.

Rnd 9: *Ssk, K2; rep from * around—27 sts.

Rnd 10: *Ssk, K1; rep from * around—18 sts.

Rnd 11: *Ssk; rep from * around—9 sts.

Cut yarn, draw through rem sts, pull tight and secure.

Finishing

Weave in ends. Block.

Furrowed Rib

A striped cap becomes anything but boring when you use two different colorways of self-striping yarn. And, since you work just two rounds of one color and then two rounds of the next, you don't need to cut and rejoin each time. Simply carry the unused yarn up as you go!

Designed by Doreen L. Marquart   Skill Level: Easy ■■□□   Size: Adult   Finished Circumference: 20" (stretches to fit)

Materials

1 skein of Jojoland Rhythm Superwash Wool (100% superwash wool; 1¾ oz; 110 yds) ④ in each of the following colors:

MC: Blooming Garden

CC: Camouflage

US size 6 (4 mm) 16" circular needle and set of 5 double-pointed needles, or size needed to obtain gauge

Stitch marker

Tapestry needle

Gauge

26 sts and 30 rows = 4" in patt

Stitch Pattern

Rnd 1: With MC, *K2, P1; rep from * around.

Rnd 2: With MC, *K1, P2; rep from * around.

Rnd 3: With CC, *K2, P1; rep from * around.

Rnd 4: With CC, *K1, P2; rep from * around.

Rep rnds 1–4 for patt.

Hat

With circular needle and MC, CO 132 sts. PM and join, being careful not to twist sts.

Work in stitch patt until hat measures 6½" from beg, ending with rnd 2 or 4.

Shape Crown

Change to dpn when needed. Maintain stripe patt as established.

Rnd 1: *(K2, P1) 3 times, K1, K2tog; rep from * around—121 sts.

Rnd 2: *(K1, P2) 3 times, K1, P1; rep from * around.

Rnd 3: *K2, P1, K1, P2tog, K2, P1, K1, P1; rep from * around—110 sts.

Rnd 4: *K1, P2, K1, P1; rep from * around.

Rnd 5: *K2, P1, K1, P1, K1, P2tog, K1, P1; rep from * around—99 sts.

Rnd 6: *K1, P2, (K1, P1) 3 times; rep from * around.

Rnd 7: *K1, P2tog, (K1, P1) 3 times; rep from * around—88 sts.

Rnd 8: *K1, P1; rep from * around.

Rnd 9: *(K1, P1) 3 times, ssk; rep from * around—77 sts.

Rnd 10: *(K1, P1) 3 times, K1; rep from * around.

Rnd 11: *K1, P1, ssk, K1, P1, K1; rep from * around—66 sts.

Rnd 12: *K1, P1, K1; rep from * around.

Rnd 13: *K1, P1, K1, ssk, K1; rep from * around—55 sts.

Rnd 14: *K1, P1, K3; rep from * around.

Rnd 15: *Ssk, K3; rep from * around—44 sts.

Rnds 16, 18, and 20: Knit.

Rnd 17: *K1, K2tog, K1; rep from * around—33 sts.

Rnd 19: *K2tog, K1; rep from * around—22 sts.

Rnd 21: *K2tog; rep from * around—11 sts.

Cut yarn, draw through rem sts, pull tight and secure.

Finishing

Weave in ends.

Parry

Super easy and right on trend, this ribbed hat will be a favorite of men and women alike. Wear it slouchy as shown, or knit fewer rounds for a snugger fit.

Materials

- 1 (1, 1) skein of Red Heart Super Saver (100% acrylic; 7 oz; 364 yds) (4) in color Medium Thyme
- US size 8 (5 mm) 16" circular needle and set of 5 double-pointed needles, or size needed to obtain gauge
- Stitch marker
- Tapestry needle

Designed by Violette Lovelace   Skill Level: Easy ■■□□   Sizes: Baby (Child, Adult)   Finished Circumference: 13½ (17¾, 22)"

Gauge

18 sts and 24 rows = 4" in St st

Hat

With circular needle, CO 60 (80, 100) sts. PM and join, being careful not to twist sts.

Work in K3, P2 rib for 45 (55, 65) rnds, or an additional 15 rnds for a fold-up brim.

Shape Crown

Divide sts evenly over 2 dpn.

Rnds 1–5: K2tog, work to 2 sts before end of first needle, P2tog; on second needle, K2tog, work to 2 sts before end of needle, P2tog—40 (60, 80) sts. Do not BO.

Finishing

Turn hat inside out. Join top seam with 3-needle BO. Weave in ends.

Smocked Beanie

Featuring a stretchy smocked pattern, *this hat is comfortable to wear and is easier to knit than it looks!*

Designed by Amy Polcyn Niezur

Skill Level: Easy ■■□□

Size: Adult

Finished Circumference: 19½" (stretches to fit)

Materials

2 skeins of Berroco Lustra (50% Peruvian wool, 50% Tencel; 3½ oz; 197 yds) **4** in color Tuileries

US size 9 (5.5 mm) 16" circular and double-pointed needles, or size needed to obtain gauge

Stitch marker

Tapestry needle

Gauge

30 sts and 22 rows = 4" in smocking patt

Smocking Pattern

Rnds 1, 2, 3, 5, 6, and 7: *K2, P2; rep from * around.

Rnd 4: *Insert right needle between 6th and 7th st on left needle, wrap around needle and pull up a loop, place loop on end of left needle (beside next st to be worked), K2tog (loop and first stitch), K1, P2, K2, P2; rep from * around.

Rnd 8: K2, P2, *insert right needle between 6th and 7th st on left needle and work as before, K2tog, K1, P2, K2, P2; rep from * around, on last rep insert right needle between 2nd and 3rd sts at beg of next rnd to complete final smocking stitch, do not move marker.

Rep rnds 1–8 for patt.

Hat

With circular needle, CO 144 sts. PM and join, being careful not to twist sts. Work even in smocking patt until piece measures 6" from beg, ending with rnd 8.

Shape Crown

Change to dpn when needed. Work dec as K2tog (P2tog when sts to be dec are both purl sts).

Rnd 1: *Work in patt over 7 sts, dec over next 2 sts; rep from * around—128 sts.

Rnd 2: Work even in patt.

Rnd 3: *Work in patt over 6 sts, dec over next 2 sts; rep from * around—112 sts.

Rnd 4: Work even in rnd 4 of patt (adjust amount of sts in each smocking group as needed to maintain patt).

Rnd 5: *Work in patt over 5 sts, dec over next 2 sts; rep from * around—96 sts.

Rnd 6: Work even in patt.

Rnd 7: *Work in patt over 4 sts, dec over next 2 sts; rep from * around—80 sts.

Rnd 8: Work even in rnd 8 of smocking patt (adjust amount of sts in each smocking group as needed to maintain patt).

Rnd 9: *Work in patt over 3 sts, dec over next 2 sts; rep from * around—64 sts.

Rnd 10: *Work in patt over 2 sts, dec over next 2 sts; rep from * around—48 sts.

Rnd 11: *Work in patt over 1 st, dec over next 2 sts; rep from * around—32 sts.

Rnd 12: *K2tog; rep from * around—16 sts.

Rnd 13: Rep rnd 12—8 sts.

Cut yarn, draw through rem sts and secure.

Finishing

Weave in ends. Block.

Openwork Swirl

Wear it when the wind is swirling the snow, on a bad hair day, or just because you want to. Whatever the weather, this comfortable swirl-top hat will provide warmth and style. This is a quick knit; cast on today and wear it tomorrow.

Designed by Sheryl Thies   Skill Level: Intermediate ■■■□   Size: Adult   Finished Circumference: 21¼"

Materials

1 skein of Zealana TUI (70% fine New Zealand merino, 15% cashmere, 15% brushtail possum; 3½ oz; 121 yds) (3) in color Red Pepper

US size 9 (5.5 mm) 16" circular needle and set of 5 double-pointed needles, or size needed to obtain gauge

Stitch marker

Tapestry needle

Gauge

15 sts = 4" in patt

Hat

With dpn, CO 8 sts, dividing evenly over 4 needles. PM and join, being careful not to twist sts. Change to circular needle when needed.

Rnds 1 and 2: Knit.

Rnd 3: *YO, K1; rep from * around—16 sts.

Rnd 4: Knit.

Rnd 5: *YO, K1; rep from * around—32 sts.

Rnd 6: *K2, K2tog; rep from * around—24 sts.

Rnd 7: *YO, K1, YO, K2tog; rep from * around—32 sts.

Rnd 8: Knit.

Rnd 9: *(YO, K1) twice, YO, K2tog; rep from * around—48 sts.

Rnd 10: *K4, K2tog; rep from * around—40 sts.

Rnd 11: *(YO, K1) 3 times, K2tog; rep from * around—56 sts.

Rnd 12: *K5, K2tog; rep from * around—48 sts.

Rnd 13: *(YO, K1) twice, YO, K2, K2tog; rep from * around—64 sts.

Rnd 14: *K6, K2tog; rep from * around—56 sts.

Rnd 15: *(YO, K1) twice, YO, K3, K2tog; rep from * around—72 sts.

Rnd 16: *K7, K2tog; rep from * around—64 sts.

Rnd 17: *(YO, K1) twice, YO, K4, K2tog; rep from * around—80 sts.

Rnd 18: *K8, K2tog; rep from * around—72 sts.

Rnd 19: *(YO, K1) twice, YO, K5, K2tog; rep from * around—88 sts.

Rnd 20: *K9, K2tog; rep from * around—80 sts.

Rnds 21 and 22: Knit.

Rnds 23, 27, and 31: *YO, K2tog; rep from * around.

Rnds 24–26 and 28–30: Knit.

Rnds 32 and 33: Knit.

Rnds 34–38: *K2, P2; rep from * around.

BO loosely in patt.

Finishing

Weave in ends. Block lightly.

Glacier

Subtle ruching lends casual elegance to this
slouchy topper, which is as easy to knit as it is easy to wear.
Decorative buttons add a fun touch.

Designed by Shana Galbraith   Skill Level: Easy ■■□□   Size: Adult   Finished Circumference: 19" (stretches to fit)

Materials

1 skein of Hobby Lobby I Love This Yarn (100% acrylic; 2½ oz; 230 yds) **3** in color Glacier

US size 7 (4.5 mm) 16" circular needle and set of 5 double-pointed needles, or size needed to obtain gauge

Stitch marker

Tapestry needle

2 buttons, ¾" diameter

Gauge

16 sts and 28 rows = 4" in St st

Hat

With circular needle, CO 76 sts. PM and join, being careful not to twist sts.

Rnd 1: *K2, P2; rep from * around.

Rnds 2–15: Rep rnd 1.

Rnd 16: *Kfb; rep from * around—152 sts.

Rnds 17–21: Knit.

Rnd 22: *K2tog; rep from * around—76 sts.

Rnds 23–27: Knit.

Rnd 28: Rep rnd 16—152 sts.

Rnds 29–33: Knit.

Rnd 34: Rep rnd 22—76 sts.

Rnds 35–39: Knit.

Rnd 40: Rep rnd 16—152 sts.

Rnds 41–45: Knit.

Rnd 46: Rep rnd 22—76 sts.

Rnd 47: Knit.

Shape Crown

Change to dpn when needed.

Rnd 1: *K5, K2tog; rep from * to last 6 sts, K6—66 sts.

Rnd 2: Knit.

Rnd 3: *K4, K2tog; rep from * around—55 sts.

Rnd 4: Knit.

Rnd 5: Rep rnd 16—110 sts.

Rnds 6–10: Knit.

Rnd 11: Rep rnd 22—55 sts.

Rnd 12: *K3, K2tog; rep from * around—44 sts.

Rnd 13: *K2, K2tog; rep from * around—33 sts.

Rnd 14: *K1, K2tog; rep from * around—22 sts.

Rnd 15: *K2tog; rep from * around—11 sts.

Cut yarn, draw through rem sts, pull tight and secure.

Finishing

Weave in ends.

Sew buttons one above the other in one of the purl sections of the ribbing of the hat.

Alphie

Combining stripes and cables adds horizontal
and vertical interest to this easy-to-knit cap. The ribbing
ensures a comfortable fit.

Designed by Violette Lovelace

Skill Level: Easy ■■□□   Size: Adult   Finished Circumference: 20"

Materials

1 skein of Red Heart Super Saver (100% acrylic; 7 oz; 364 yds) **4** in each of the following colors:

MC: Black

CC: Grey Heather

US size 3 (3.25 mm) 16" circular needle and set of 5 double-pointed needles, or size needed to obtain gauge

Cable needle

Stitch marker

Tapestry needle

Gauge

22 sts = 4" in patt

Special Abbreviation

C6B: Slip 3 sts to cable needle and hold in back, K3, K3 from cable needle.

Hat

With circular needle and MC, cast on 112 sts. PM and join, being careful not to twist sts. Work in K2, P2 rib for 40 rnds. Change to CC. Work in K2, P2 rib for 1 rnd. Beg patt as follows:

Rnd 1: *K6, P2; rep from * around.

Rnds 2–7: Rep rnd 1.

Rnd 8: *C6B, P2, K6, P2; rep from * around.

Rnds 9–12: Rep rnd 1. Change to MC.

Rnds 13–22: Rep rnd 1.

Rnd 23: Rep rnd 8.

Rnds 24–27: Rep rnd 1. Change to CC.

Rnds 28–30: Rep rnd 1.

Shape Crown

Change to dpn when needed.

Rnd 1: *K6, P2tog around; rep from * around—98 sts.

Rnd 2: *K6, P1; rep from * around.

Rnd 3: *K5, K2tog; rep from * around—84 sts.

Rnds 4, 6, 8, and 10: Knit.

Rnd 5: *K4, K2tog; rep from * around—70 sts.

Rnd 7: *K3, K2tog; rep from * around—56 sts.

Rnd 9: *K2, K2tog; rep from * around—42 sts.

Rnd 11: *K1, K2tog; rep from * around—28 sts.

Rnd 12: *K2tog; rep from * around—14 sts.

Cut yarn, draw through rem sts, pull tight and secure.

Finishing

Weave in ends.

Gimme a Kiss

Worked in the round *from the brim up, this hat's brim stays securely in place after it's folded up with accent buttons. Simple cable stitches combine to make a clever X and O design, also known as Hugs and Kisses.*

Designed by Shana Galbraith   Skill Level: Intermediate ■■■□   Size: Adult   Finished Circumference: 22½"

Materials

1 skein of Lion Brand Vanna's Choice (100% acrylic; 3½ oz; 170 yds) (4) in color Magenta

US size 7 (4.5 mm) 16" circular needle and set of 5 double-pointed needles, or size needed to obtain gauge

Cable needle

Stitch marker

Tapestry needle

2 buttons, ¾" diameter

Gauge

17 sts and 28 rows = 4" in rib patt

Special Abbreviations

C4F: Slip 2 sts to cable needle and hold in front, K2, K2 from cable needle.

C4B: Slip 2 sts to cable needle and hold in back, K2, K2 from cable needle.

C3F: Slip 1 st to cable needle and hold in front, K2, K1 from cable needle.

T2B: Slip 1 st to cable needle and hold in back, K1, K1 from cable needle.

Hat

With circular needle, CO 96 sts. PM and join, being careful not to twist sts.

Rnd 1: *K1, P1; rep from * around.

Rnds 2–13: Rep rnd 1.

Rnd 14: *K2, Kfb; rep from * around—128 sts.

Rnd 15: Knit.

Rnd 16: *C4B, (C4F) twice, C4B; rep from * around.

Rnds 17–19: Knit.

Rnd 20: Rep rnd 16.

Rnds 21–23: Knit.

Rnd 24: *C4F, (C4B) twice, C4F; rep from * around.

Rnds 25–27: Knit.

Rnd 28: Rep rnd 24.

Rnds 29 and 30: Knit.

Rnds 31–46: Rep rnds 15–30.

Rnd 47: Rep rnd 15.

Rnd 48: Rep rnd 16.

Rnd 49: Rep rnd 17.

Rnd 50: Rep rnd 18.

Shape Crown

Change to dpn when needed.

Rnd 1: *K4, (K2tog, K2) twice, K4; rep from * around—112 sts.

Rnd 2: *C4B, (C3F) twice, C4B; rep from * around.

Rnd 3: Knit.

Rnd 4: *K4, (K1, K2tog) twice, K4; rep from * around—96 sts.

Rnd 5: Knit.

Rnd 6: *C4F, (T2B) twice, C4F; rep from * around.

Rnd 7: *K4, (K2tog) twice, K4; rep from * around—80 sts.

Rnd 8: *K2tog; rep from * around—40 sts.

Rnd 9: *K2tog; rep from * around—20 sts.

Cut yarn, draw through rem sts, pull tight and secure.

Finishing

With tail from CO, tack bottom of brim up at back of hat, ½" above top of rib. Sew buttons in place as shown, one on each side, approx 10" apart. Weave in ends.

Faith

Bulky yarn and tweedy texture combine to create a hat that's perfect for casual walks in the park on a crisp fall day. Large needles mean a quick knit.

Designed by Shana Galbraith

Skill Level: Easy ■■□□

Size: Adult

Finished Circumference: 20"

Materials

1 skein of Lion Brand Wool-Ease Thick and Quick (86% acrylic, 10% wool, 4% rayon; 6 oz; 106 yds) (6) in color Wheat

US size 11 (8 mm) 16" circular needle and set of 5 double-pointed needles, or size needed to obtain gauge

Stitch marker

Tapestry needle

Gauge

8 sts and 16 rows = 4" in rib patt

Adjusting Size

To make a child-size hat, use a chunky-weight yarn, such as Lion Brand Wool Ease Chunky and size 10 (6 mm) needles, and work remainder of pattern as written.

Hat

With circular needle, CO 40 sts. PM and join, being careful not to twist sts.

Rnd 1: *K2, P2; rep from * around.

Rnds 2–10: Rep rnd 1.

Rnd 11: *P3, Pfb, P4; rep from * around—45 sts.

Rnd 12: Purl to last st, Pfb, in last st—46 sts.

Rnds 13–15: Purl.

Rnds 16–20: *K2, P2; rep from * around to last 2 sts, K2.

Rnds 21–25: Purl.

Rnds 26–30: Rep rnds 16–20.

Rnd 31: Purl.

Rnd 32: *P7, P2tog; rep from * around, end last rep P3tog—40 sts.

Rnds 33–35: Purl.

Rnds 36 and 37: *K2, P2; rep from * around.

Shape Crown

Change to dpn when needed.

Rnd 1: *K2, P2tog, K2, P2; rep from * around—35 sts.

Rnd 2: *K2, P1, K2, P2tog; rep from * around—30 sts.

Rnd 3: *K1, K2tog; rep from * around—20 sts.

Rnd 4: *K2tog; rep from * around—10 sts.

Cut yarn, draw through rem sts, pull tight and secure.

Finishing

Weave in ends.

Big-Needle Duo

If you're looking for a quick project, you've found it!
Big needles (size 19) make fast work of knitting one skein
of yarn. Plan to make more than one set—this pair makes a
great gift and is perfect for charitable giving, too.

Designed by Violette Lovelace

Skill Level: Beginner ■□□□

Size: Adult   Finished Circumference: 22"

Materials

1 skein of Loops and Threads Zoomba (100% acrylic; 5 oz; 114 yds) (6) in color Rapid

US size 19 (15 mm) straight needles, or size needed to obtain gauge

Tapestry needle

Gauge

5 sts and 7 rows = 4" in St st

Hat

CO 28 sts.

Rows 1 (WS)–7: Knit.

Rows 8–15: Work in St st.

Row 16: P1, P2tog, P4, P2tog, P4, P2tog, P4, P2tog, P4, P2tog, P1—23 sts.

Rows 17, 19, 21, and 23: Knit.

Row 18: P1, P2tog, P3, P2tog, P3, P2tog, P3, P2tog, P3, P2tog—18 sts.

Row 20: P1, P2tog, P2, P2tog, P2, P2tog, P2, P2tog, P3—14 sts.

Row 22: P2tog, P1, P2tog, P1, P2tog, P1, P2tog, P1, P2tog—9 sts.

Row 24: P2tog, P2tog, P1, P2tog, P2tog—5 sts.

Cut yarn, draw through rem sts, pull tight and secure.

Finishing

Sew back seam. Weave in ends. Block lightly.

Scarf

With leftover yarn, CO 10 sts. Work in K1, P1 rib until only 18" of yarn rem. BO in patt. Weave in ends.

Curly-Q Beret

A saucy beret in a cheerful berry hue is just the thing to brighten up a bleak winter day. You can make quick work of this hat and finish it in just one evening.

Designed by Violette Lovelace

Skill Level: Easy ■■□□

Size: Adult

Finished Circumference: 19" (stretches to fit)

Materials

1 skein of Lion Brand Hometown USA (100% acrylic; 5 oz; 81 yds) (6) in color New Orleans French Berry

US size 15 (10 mm) 16" circular needle and set of 5 double-pointed needles, or size needed to obtain gauge

Stitch marker

Tapestry needle

Gauge

7½ sts and 10 rows = 4" in St st

Special Technique

I-Cord: With dpn, *knit 1 row; without turning work, slide sts to right end of needle; rep from * until cord measures desired length.

Hat

With circular needle, CO 36 sts. PM and join, being careful not to twist sts.

Rnds 1–3: *K1, P1; rep from * around.

Rnds 4–8: Knit.

Rnd 9: *K1, Kfb; rep from * around—54 sts.

Rnds 10–17: Knit.

Shape Crown

Change to dpn when needed.

Rnd 1: *K7, ssk; rep from * around—48 sts.

Rnd 2: *K6, ssk; rep from * around—42 sts.

Rnd 3: *K5, ssk; rep from * around—36 sts.

Rnd 4: *K10, ssk; rep from * around—33 sts.

Rnd 5: *K9, ssk; rep from * around—30 sts.

Rnd 6: *K8, ssk; rep from * around—27 sts.

Rnd 7: *K7, ssk; rep from * around—24 sts.

Rnd 8: *K6, ssk; rep from * around—21 sts.

Rnd 9: *K5, ssk; rep from * around—18 sts.

Rnd 10: *K4, ssk; rep from * around—15 sts.

Rnd 11: *K3, ssk; rep from * around—12 sts.

Rnd 12: *K2, ssk; rep from * around—9 sts.

Rnd 13: *K1, ssk; rep from * around—6 sts.

Rnd 14: *Ssk; rep from * around—3 sts.

Work I-cord for 3 to 7 rows or to length desired.

Next row: Ssk, K1—2 sts. Bind off.

Finishing

Weave in ends. Block. If desired, sew end of I-cord to base of I-cord to form a loop.

Fair Isle Roll

This is a great quick-knit hat—perfect for a first Fair Isle project! You only need three colors, so stranding won't be too complicated, and this hat is just the right size for practicing—and finishing—colorwork knitting.

Designed by Doreen L. Marquart   Skill Level: Intermediate ■■■□   Size: Adult Small (Large)   Finished Circumference: 19 (22½)"

Materials

1 skein of Berroco Vintage (50% acrylic, 40% wool, 10% nylon; 3½ oz; 217 yds) 〔4〕 in each of the following colors:

MC: Mocha

A: Oats

B: Aquae

US size 7 (4.5 mm) 16" circular needle and set of 5 double-pointed needles, or size needed to obtain gauge

Stitch marker

Tapestry needle

Gauge

20 sts and 28 rows = 4" in St st

Stitch Pattern

See chart at right.

Hat

With circular needle and MC, CO 96 (112) sts. PM and join, being careful not to twist sts. Work in St st for 4".

Work 19 rnds of chart.

With MC, work in St st until piece measures 9 (10)" from beg, unrolled.

Shape Crown

Change to dpn when needed.

Rnd 1: K6, *sl 2-K1-psso, K13; rep from * around, ending last rep K7—84 (98) sts.

Rnd 2 and all even-numbered rnds: Knit.

Rnd 3: K5, *sl 2-K1-psso, K11; rep from * around, ending last rep K6—72 (84) sts.

Rnd 5: K4, *sl 2-K1-psso, K9; rep from * around, ending last rep K5—60 (70) sts.

Rnd 7: K3, *sl 2-K1-psso, K7; rep from * around, ending last rep K4—48 (56) sts.

Rnd 9: K2, *sl 2-K1-psso, K5; rep from * around, ending last rep K3—36 (42) sts.

Rnd 11: K1, *sl 2-K1-psso, K3; rep from * around, ending last rep K2—24 (28) sts.

Rnd 13: *Sl 2-K1-psso, K1; rep from * around—12 (14) sts.

Rnd 15: K2tog around—6 (7) sts.

Cut yarn, draw through rem sts, pull tight and secure.

Finishing

Weave in ends.

Fair Isle Roll

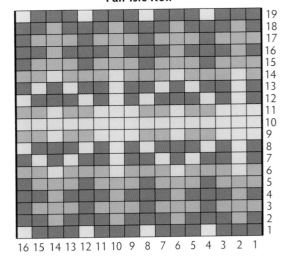

Repeat = 16 sts

Legend

■ MC: Mocha

□ A: Oats

■ B: Aquae

Colorwork

With only one color per round, this fun design
works up with no need to strand the yarn!

Designed by Amy Polcyn Niezur   Skill Level: Easy ■■□□   Size: Adult   Finished Circumference: 19½" (stretches to fit)

Materials

1 skein of Classic Elite Liberty Wool (100% washable wool; 1¾ oz; 122 yds) (**4**) in each of the following colors:

MC: Slate

CC: Wine

US size 7 (4.5 mm) straight, 16" circular and double-pointed needles, or size needed to obtain gauge

Stitch marker

Tapestry needle

Gauge

19 sts and 28 rows = 4" in St st

Stitch Pattern

See chart on page 56.

Note

Stitch count is increased for colorwork pattern due to difference in gauge. Colorwork pattern is worked back and forth in rows, slipping all sts purlwise.

Hat

With straight needles and MC, CO 94 sts. Do not join. Work in K2, P2 rib, ending with K2, for 1½", ending with a WS row.

Next row (RS): With MC, knit, inc 11 sts evenly across—105 sts.

Work rows 2–20 of chart once, then work rows 1 and 2 once more.

With MC, change to circular needle, PM and join. Work in St st until piece measures 6" from beg, dec 11 sts evenly on first rnd—94 sts.

Shape Crown

Change to dpn when needed.

Rnd 1: Knit, dec 4 sts evenly around—90 sts.

Rnd 2: *K7, K2tog; rep from * around—80 sts.

Rnds 3, 5, 7, 9, 11, and 13: Knit.

Rnd 4: *K6, K2tog; rep from * around—70 sts.

Rnd 6: *K5, K2tog; rep from * around—60 sts.

Rnd 8: *K4, K2tog; rep from * around—50 sts.

Rnd 10: *K3, K2tog; rep from * around—40 sts.

Rnd 12: *K2, K2tog; rep from * around—30 sts.

Rnd 14: *K1, K2tog; rep from * around—20 sts.

Rnd 15: *K2tog; rep from * around—10 sts.

Rnd 16: *K2tog; rep from * around—5 sts.

Cut yarn, draw through rem sts and secure.

Finishing

Sew center back seam. Weave in ends. Block.

Colorwork

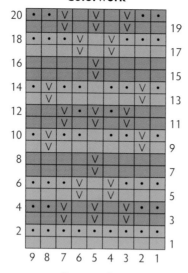

Row numbers on left: 20, 18, 16, 14, 12, 10, 8, 6, 4, 2
Row numbers on right: 19, 17, 15, 13, 11, 9, 7, 5, 3, 1

Stitch numbers (bottom): 9 8 7 6 5 4 3 2 1

Repeat = 9 sts

Legend

with MC, K on RS, P on WS	with CC, P on RS, K on WS
with CC, K on RS, P on WS	V Sl 1 with MC at WS of work
with MC, P on RS, K on WS	V Sl 1 with CC at WS of work

Damask

The subtle floral design of this colorwork cap
evokes the delicate damask fabrics of yesteryear.

Designed by Sharon E. Mooney

Skill Level: Intermediate ■■■□

Size: Adult

Finished Circumference: 21¾"

Materials

1 skein of Patons Classic Wool DK Superwash (100% pure new wool; 1¾ oz; 125 yds) **3** in each of the following colors:

MC: Dark Grey Heather

CC: Medium Grey Heather

US size 4 (3.5 mm) 16" circular needle and set of 5 double-pointed needles, or size needed to obtain gauge

Stitch marker

Tapestry needle

Scrap of cardboard, 3" long

Gauge

22 sts and 26 rows = 4" in St st

Stitch Pattern

See chart on page 59.

Hat

With circular needle and MC, CO 120 sts. PM and join, being careful not to twist sts.

Rnd 1: With MC, purl.

Rnd 2: *With MC, K2; with CC, K2; rep from * around.

Rnd 3: *With MC, K2; with CC, P2; rep from * around.

Rnds 4–7: Rep rnd 2.

Rnd 8: With MC, knit.

Rnd 9: With MC, purl.

Work chart (rep chart sts 3 times each rnd), changing to dpn when needed—18 sts.

Cut yarn, draw through rem sts, pull tight and secure.

Finishing

Weave in ends. Block.

Pom-Pom

Wrap 1 strand of each yarn, held together, approx 100 times around a scrap of 3"-long cardboard. Tie firmly around center on each side, slide off cardboard, tie both pieces together in center, and cut loops at each end. Tie entire piece together in center, trim ends, and fluff. Sew pom-pom to top of hat.

Damask

Legend

- K in MC
- ☐ K in CC
- ⟋ K2tog
- ⟍ Ssk
- ■ No st

Techniques

Refer to the following instructions if you need help with general knitting techniques.

Basic Pattern Stitches

Most of the designs in this book are knit using either garter stitch or stockinette stitch.

Garter Stitch

In the round: Knit odd-numbered rounds; purl even-numbered rounds.

Stockinette Stitch

In the round: Knit every round.

Casting On

When casting on for ribbing on a hat, choose a cast on that is stretchy enough to make it easy to put the hat on and will keep it snug. If a particular cast on isn't called for, you can simply use your favorite method. After casting on, join stitches to work in the round, as instructed, being careful not to twist them when you join them.

Increasing

While there are numerous methods of increasing stitches, the following are the recommended methods for the designs in this book.

Knit in Front and Back of Stitch (Kfb)

This stitch is one of the most basic and easiest ways to increase. You simply knit into the stitch you want to increase in as you normally would, only don't take the stitch off of either needle.

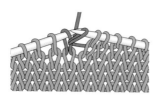

Now, bring the right needle around to the back of your work and knit that same stitch again, this time going into the back loop of the stitch you are increasing in.

This type of increase will result in one normal-looking stitch while the other stitch will have a horizontal bar going across it. Usually this little bar doesn't cause any problems, but on occasion it does take away from the look of the garment, and you may want to opt for a different increase method.

Make One (M1)

Another way to increase stitches is to work a "make one" increase. This increase is virtually invisible.

Work up to the point where the increase is called for. Pick up the horizontal bar between the stitch just worked and the next stitch by inserting the left needle from front to back and placing the acquired loop on the left needle. Now, you'll simply knit this stitch through the back loop.

You'll notice that you are actually twisting the stitch as you knit it. If you don't twist the stitch, you'll get a hole where the bar was picked up. By knitting into the back of the stitch, you'll eliminate the hole.

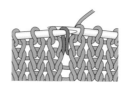

Pick up the horizontal bar.

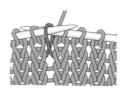

Knit into the back of the stitch.

Decreasing

Most of the decreases in this book are made with the simplest knit two together, which is a right-slanting decrease. Sometimes, however, you'll need a right-slanting slip, slip, knit decrease.

Knit Two Together (K2tog)

When completed, the stitch will slant toward the right. Instead of knitting the next stitch on the left needle, simply insert the right-hand needle from left to right through both the second stitch and the first stitch on the left-hand needle. Knit them together as one stitch.

Slip, Slip, Knit (ssk)

When completed, the stitch will slant to the left. It's a mirror image of the knit-two-together decrease. Work to where the decrease is to be made. Slip the next two stitches individually, as if to knit, to the right-hand needle. Insert your left-hand needle into the front part of these stitches, from top to bottom, and knit these two stitches together, making one stitch.

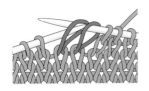 

I-Cord

I-cord is a wonderful way to make drawstrings and ties for your knitted items. The width of I-cord is determined by the number of cast-on stitches and the weight of yarn you are using. The pattern will specify how many stitches to use.

Using double-pointed needles in the same size as you used for the hat (unless the pattern specifies differently), cast on the number of stitches specified in the pattern. Knit all of the stitches, but *do not* turn work. Place the needle with the stitches in your left hand and slide the stitches back to the opposite end of the needle. Knit the stitches again, making sure the yarn is pulled snugly when it's brought from the last stitch worked in the previous row to the first stitch worked in this row. Do not turn work. Continue to slide the stitches to the opposite end of the needle and knit them. The yarn is pulled across the back each time to start the new row. After working three to four rows, you'll see a cord being formed.

If the cord is loose, it's most likely because the yarn isn't pulled tightly across the back when beginning each row.

Kitchener Stitch

The Kitchener stitch is a type of grafting used to join two pieces of knitting together. It's done by creating a row of knitting by hand with a tapestry needle and is completely flat and invisible when correctly done. Kitchener stitch is often used to close the toe of socks or, as in this case, the top opening of a hat.

Place half of the stitches to be joined on one needle and the other half on a second needle, the same size as your project needles.

Hold the needles together in your left hand with the *wrong* sides of the work together. Thread a piece of yarn long enough to work your stitches onto a tapestry needle. Make sure you have enough yarn so you don't run out partway through.

First stitch

Front needle: Insert the tapestry needle as if to purl that stitch, leave the stitch on the knitting needle, and pull the yarn through.

Back needle: Insert the tapestry needle as if to knit that stitch, leave the stitch on the knitting needle, and pull the yarn through.

Remainder of Row to Last Stitch

Front needle: Insert the tapestry needle as if to knit the first stitch and slip it off the knitting needle onto the tapestry needle. Immediately go through the next stitch on the front needle as if to purl, leaving it on the knitting needle, and pull the yarn through.

Back needle: Insert the tapestry needle as if to purl the first stitch and slip it off the knitting needle onto the tapestry needle. Immediately go through the next stitch on the back needle as if to knit, leaving it on the knitting needle, and pull the yarn through.

Last Stitch

Front needle: Insert the tapestry needle as if to knit the stitch and slip it off the knitting needle.

Back needle: Insert the tapestry needle as if to purl the stitch, slip it off the knitting needle, and pull the yarn through.

Weave in the yarn tail on the wrong side.

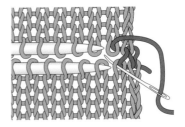

Helpful Information

Standard Yarn-Weight System

Yarn-Weight Symbol and Category Name	**1** Super Fine	**2** Fine	**3** Light	**4** Medium	**5** Bulky	**6** Super Bulky
Types of Yarn in Category	Sock, Fingering, Baby	Sport, Baby	DK, Light Worsted	Worsted, Afghan, Aran	Chunky, Craft, Rug	Bulky, Roving
Knit Gauge Range* in Stockinette Stitch to 4"	27 to 32 sts	23 to 26 sts	21 to 24 sts	16 to 20 sts	12 to 15 sts	6 to 11 sts
Recommended Needle in Metric Size Range	2.25 to 3.25 mm	3.25 to 3.75 mm	3.75 to 4.5 mm	4.5 to 5.5 mm	5.5 to 8 mm	8 mm and larger
Recommended Needle in US Size Range	1 to 3	3 to 5	5 to 7	7 to 9	9 to 11	11 and larger

*These are guidelines only. The above reflect the most commonly used gauges and needle sizes for specific yarn categories.

Metric Conversions

Yds	=	meters	x	1.0936
Meters	=	yds	x	0.9144
Ounces	=	grams	x	0.0352
Grams	=	ounces	x	28.35

Abbreviations and Glossary

approx	approximately
beg	begin(ning)
BO	bind off
CC	contrasting color
CO	cast on
dec	decrease(ing)(s)
dpn	double-pointed needle(s)
g	gram(s)
inc	increase(ing)(s)
K	knit
Kfb	knit into the front and the back of the next stitch—1 stitch increased
K2tog	knit 2 stitches together—1 stitch decreased
K2tog tbl	knit 2 stitches together through the back loops—1 stitch decreased
K3tog	knit three stitches together—2 stitches decreased
M1	make 1 stitch—1 stitch increased
M1L	make 1 stitch left
M1R	make 1 stitch right
MC	main color
mm	millimeter(s)
oz	ounce(s)

P	purl
P2tog	purl 2 stitches together—1 stitch decreased
P3tog	purl 3 stitches together—2 stitches decreased
patt	pattern
Pfb	purl into the front and the back of the next stitch—1 stitch increased
PM	place marker
psso	pass slipped st(s) over
rem	remain(ing)
rep	repeat(ing)
rnd(s)	round(s)
RS	right side
sl 1	slip 1 stitch
ssk	slip 2 stitches knitwise, 1 at a time, to right needle, then insert left needle from left to right into front loops and knit 2 stitches together—1 stitch decreased
st(s)	stitch(es)
St st	stockinette stitch
tbl	through back loop(s)
tog	together
WS	wrong side
yds	yards
YO	yarn over

Meet the Designers

Jessica Anderson has five wonderful kids and one very supportive husband. She started knitting about eight years ago when her husband thought it was silly to spend $60 on a pair of knitted pants to cover their little one's cloth diapers. (He since realizes that was a bargain compared to how much she spends on knitting tools and yarn!) When she isn't knitting, Jessica juggles homeschooling, sharing coffee with friends, and studying to be a homebirth midwife. Her designs can be found on Ravelry (her username is MonkeyButtBabies), Craftsy, and in various knitting publications. She blogs at allinadaysfun.blogspot.com.

Violette Lovelace, who can be found at her online shop, Knit Kritters on etsy, has been knitting for over a dozen years. She started her shop while in high school when she wanted to help her friends raise funds for a choir trip by selling scarves. Now she sells her scarves, blankets, toys, and costumes online and at comic conventions. In her spare time, she likes to crochet, draw, and cosplay (costumed role play). She is always looking for new creative things to make.

Shana Galbraith learned to crochet as a child, and was quickly fascinated by chains and granny squares. In 2009, she picked up knitting as part of her recovery from OCD, and found she loved knitting even more. She makes a living from her fiber antics, and her sofa often seats more yarn than people. Her second love is fitness and nutrition, and she loves creating healthy versions of comfort foods. She resides with her three children in Idaho and dreams of one day having a studio full of yarn on a tropical island. You can find more of her patterns at yarntwisted.etsy.com.

David Owen Hastings is a Pacific Northwest graphic designer and artist and has been knitting for decades, since he was about eight years old. In his design office, he works exclusively with nonprofit organizations to help with their branding and communications projects. In his fine art studio, he creates organic abstractions, inspired by nature and the elements. David brings his love of color and texture to every knitted project and has made countless beanies for friends' and family members' babies. Learn more about David at davidowenhastings.com.

Jen Lucas has been knitting since 2004 and designing since 2008. She is shawl-obsessed and is the author of the popular *Sock-Yarn Shawls* books. Her designs have been seen in several magazines, including *Interweave Knits* and *Knitscene*. You can also find dozens of her self-published patterns on Ravelry. She lives in Fox River Grove, Illinois, with her husband, Alex. Visit Jen at jenlucasdesigns.com.

Megan Kreiner comes from a long line of knitters and crocheters. She learned the craft at an early age from her grandmother, her aunt, and her mother. As of 2012, her MK Crochet pattern line has been published and featured in books and various crochet and knitting magazines. A graduate with a fine arts degree in computer graphics and animation from the University of Massachusetts, Amherst, Megan currently works as an animator at DreamWorks Animation. Megan lives in Altadena, California, with her husband, Michael, and their children, James and Emily. View her work at MKCrochet.com.

Doreen L. Marquart, of Delavan, Wisconsin, taught herself to knit at the age of nine and has been knitting ever since. In 1993, she opened Needles 'n Pins Yarn Shoppe, which is now the largest shop in her area devoted exclusively to the needs of knitters and crocheters. Doreen has published six books with Martingale. She also has many individual patterns that are available on Ravelry. Visit Doreen online at needlesnpinsyarnshoppe.com.

Sharon E. Mooney has been knitting since before she could read and has worked in two yarn shops and owned two others. She has designed for many yarn companies and has patterns published in magazines and books. She's also had designs featured in fashion shows at both Stitches West and TNNA events. She has coauthored a lace-knitting book as well. Sharon lives in and loves southern California.

Amy Polcyn Niezur has been designing professionally since 2005, with over 275 patterns published in magazines, books, and yarn-company collections. She is also the author of two knitting books. When not knitting, Amy is out for a run. She has completed several marathons and regularly wins her age group in 5K events. Additionally, she loves the aerial arts and spends an alarming amount of time upside down. Amy lives in suburban Detroit with her husband, dog, and teenage daughter. Find out more at amypolcyn.com.

Sheryl Thies retired from a career in healthcare to follow her artistic passion—combining fiber, texture, and color. This pursuit led to teaching opportunities both near and far, from local yarn shops to international waters aboard cruise ships. She is the author of both knitting and Tunisian crochet books including best-selling *Get Hooked on Tunisian Crochet* and her latest book, *Slip-Stitch Knits*. In addition to designing and teaching, she enjoys spending time outdoors and can often be found on the bocce court, either playing of refereeing.